BUT OUR PRINCESS IS IN ANOTHER CASTLE

ADVANCE PRAISE

"In *But Our Princess Is in Another Castle*, B.J. Best pushes into our ribs and digs through our childhoods—the hands we held, the red of our first kiss, the skin we've shed and calloused from every game controller—until we can taste the dust we inhaled while blowing on a Super Nintendo cartridge that wouldn't work properly. With *But Our Princess*, Best has written an engrossing, personal, and highly addictive collection of poetry. He has reminded us why it's such a good time to be reading contemporary poetry. This is a book meant to be read on weekdays—a eulogy for those too bright mornings when you would try to get Cloud past the first disc of *FFVII* before your mom would tear the controller from your hands and drag you off to school. Early in *But Our Princess*, Best writes, 'What left, but to build again.' After finishing the collection, I was left with my own thoughts: What left, but to read it again? Then: Thank God books come with reset buttons."

—GREGORY SHERL, author of *The Oregon Trail Is the Oregon Trail*

BUT OUR PRINCESS IS IN ANOTHER CASTLE

Prose Poems by **B.J. BEST**

Rose Metal Press

2013

Rose Metal Press, Inc.
P.O. Box 1956
Brookline, MA 02446
rosemetalpress@gmail.com
www.rosemetalpress.com

Library of Congress Control Number: 2013930043

ISBN: 978-0-9846166-8-8

Cover and interior design by Heather Butterfield
    For more information about the typefaces used, please see "A Note about the Type" on page 92.
Cover art by Sarah James of Patsy Fine Design
    More information and artwork can be viewed on the artist's website: www.patsyfine.com.

All games, characters, and trademarks referenced in this book are the properties of their respective companies. Neither B.J. Best nor Rose Metal Press is affiliated in any way with any of these games or their companies. For further information, please see "Games Referenced" on page 87.

This book is manufactured in the United States of America and printed on acid-free paper.

MIX
Paper from
responsible sources
FSC www.fsc.org **FSC® C011935**

TABLE OF CONTENTS

4. HEART WORLD

5. DO WORLD

6. MIND WORLD

ACKNOWLEDGMENTS

Grateful acknowledgment is given to the editors of the following publications in which these poems first appeared, sometimes in slightly different versions:

Backwards City Review: "The Legend of Zelda"
Blue Earth Review: "Where in the Retirement Home Is Carmen Sandiego?"
Blue Mesa Review: "Psalm: GoldenEye 007"
Cake: "Marble Madness"
Cavalier Literary Couture: "Kid Icarus"
Cream City Review: "Asteroids," "Grand Theft Auto: Vice City," "Perfect Dark," "Rad Racer," "Sinistar," "Super Mario Bros."
Dislocate: "Mega Man," "The Oregon Trail"
Epicenter: "God Plays Tetris"
Hayden's Ferry Review: "Loom"
Pear Noir!: "Bubble Bobble," "Commander Keen," "Gauntlet"
Permafrost: "Teenage Mutant Ninja Turtles"
Pleiades: "Ms. and Super Pac-Man"
Sentence: "Pac-Man"
Southeast Review: "King's Quest"
Specs: "Altered Beast," "Golden Axe," "Space Invaders"
Sugar House Review: "Qix"
Terminus: "Our Year in Atari"
Timber: "Excitebike," "Mr. Do!," "Rampage"
Ugly Accent: "Grim Fandango"

The title of the book is a quote from *Super Mario Bros.* (Kyoto: Nintendo, 1985.)

The epigraph is from *Lucky Wander Boy* by D.B. Weiss. (New York: Plume, 2003. 8.)

The quoted line in "Maniac Mansion" is from "Silence" by Marianne Moore. (*Complete Poems*. New York: Penguin Books, 1994. 91.)

The quoted line in "Dig Dug" is from "Northern Pike" by James Wright. (*Above the River: The Complete Poems*. Wesleyan University Press edition. New York: Farrar, Straus and Giroux, 1992. 217.)

The quoted lines in "Smash TV" are from the theme songs for *The Facts of Life* (written by Al Burton, Gloria Loring, and Alan Thicke; performed by Gloria Loring) and *Mr. Belvedere* (written by Judy Hart-Angelo and Gary Portnoy; performed by Leon Redbone).

Many thanks: To Sam Barsanti for some marketing cheat codes. To Phong Nguyen for publishing six of these poems in *Cream City Review*, along with an interview and artist's statement about them. To Michael Kriesel and Erik Richardson for manuscript advice. To Melissa McGraw for manuscript advice as well as comments on first drafts of many of these poems, despite having never played most of the games—in some ways, an ideal reader. To Joshua Beam, Michael Christian, Rob Eckert, and Charles Nevsimal for their brotherhood. To my parents who, among many other things, purchased my first Nintendo in 1986. And to Erin and Henry for their love.

There is a world beneath the glass that we can never know.

—D.B. Weiss
Lucky Wander Boy

THE STORY

GOLDEN AXE

I am journeying because someone has died. In Utah, every steeple bleeds bees. The corners of my suitcase ache. Do not believe me.

The mane of an eagle. A turtle's scabbed back. The squeakiness of thieves. A serpent eating the tail of a cat eating the tail of a mouse eating the tail of a kite. Do not believe me.

BEGINNING WORLD

COMMANDER KEEN

We were raised in the decade of crashed spaceships. We'd see them from the school bus: one would be large as a car wreck, coughing purple smoke. Another was small as a crushed can, glinting in the gravel.

Science class was only good for answers. We learned space is a vacuum, blank as a bubble. We guessed licking a nine-volt battery was like tasting champagne. A hawk ate a snake ate a mouse ate some grain. Mars stared at us from page 63, red as a kickball.

It was fall. We were building a fort in the woods, laying out branches like an electrical diagram drawn in crayon. All those leaves. We kept twin imaginary robots that looked like ordinary flashlights. One was named Terror. The other was Fear. The weatherman made frost sound like a mystery, but we learned it was just the natural progression of things—water getting older, harder, more bitter. We had a backpack filled with fruit snacks, beef jerky, and our mothers' cameras.

We would be ready. We would be ready for when they came.

SIMCITY

In my sandbox lived a family of earthmovers. A Tonka dump truck, yellow as a dandelion. A bulldozer flecked with rust, its scoop the size of my palm. Together, they had children: a plastic crane with a winch strung with dental floss, Hot Wheels that emerged from the sand as if hatched from eggs.

The cities my brother and I would build there! Castles with turrets, buttresses, balustrades. Rows of square cottages with streets carved like canyons between them. Parks dotted with clover. And the massive wheel of a power plant churning when someone would fill its funnel from above. The whole thing powered by sand.

What left, but to destroy it. An apocalypse of plastic horses, their hooves grinding grains to glass. Or helicopters falling dead from the sky. Or a battalion of army men performing reconnaissance, sniping at shovels, fighting from foxholes. Their grenades of acorns were simply too much.

Eventually, we were called inside, pork chops and applesauce. Eventually, rain would finish our ruin, leaving hummocks and craters that may as well have been on the moon. The trucks glistening like rovers.

What left, but to build again.

SUPER MARIO BROS.

I.

Clearly, Luigi is the younger brother. It is Mario who is first in the sewers, who is unperturbed by the lethal squid, who can blast fire through that brickscape in front of rolling green hills. In a two-player game, no one ever chooses to be Luigi, unless they are trying to be dimly countercultural about it, like drinking Pepsi instead of Coke. But it is your machine, and you are Mario, breaking each secret block hung impossible in the air, and your friend is Luigi, so green in his hand-me-down overalls, and your friend does not have a machine, diving into obvious pits and serving suicide to oversized carnivorous plants. At the end of the level, he is so exhausted he is not sure he wants to drag himself into that castle.

II.

We were playing a game where one of us stood behind the shed door and peeked out while the other stood twenty feet away and threw rocks, trying to hit the person behind the door. It was a game, the rocks were small, and we traded roles often. Finally, my head edging out, your rock struck just above my temple, and I momentarily blacked out, then started bawling. Mom came out, found you were throwing rocks, began yelling—"Why are you throwing rocks! You could have killed him!" etc.—and you were resoundingly punished.

I did not come to your defense.

III.

Luigi sold out his share of the plumbing business a while ago—"Send the monkey wrenches back to the monkeyhouse," he would joke—and has opened up an Italian restaurant where he is, if not happy, at least content. He is proud of his pizzas, expertly spinning the dough in the air. Mario is on temporary leave from his job (his apprentices all plenty precocious), which many believe will soon become permanent. He rattles around his house, sleeping in fractures, often not long enough to dream, but when he does he is back in those comfortable caverns: ah familiarity, stars and flowers, and he is excellent and navigates with ease. Dutifully, each night, dazzling drugs leap into his mouth, streaking in arcs when he flips the lid of the pill bottle off with his thumb.

KID ICARUS

I. UNDERWORLD

Why you, post-retirement, had a Nintendo was beyond me. For *Duck Hunt*, sure; you even painted and modified the sights of the gun for better aim. You shot at the dog, just like I did, when he mocked you.

But this game made no sense: smiling snakes and red eyeball-things, and you a fruity, flying angel. "Icky Kid," you called it, as I sat on your living room floor ascending the levels with grade school ease.

II. OVERWORLD

Later, you stood on the pier, searching for muskie and twirling the reel. Through fishing, your hands had learned grace: the weight of the rod, the skein of a net, even how to tie jigs—a pink head with white-feathered body, you found, worked best.

My brother watched behind you, unaware. You flipped the rod back and a hook caught his ear; then you rolled your wrist forward in the arc of a cast. After the expected hysterics and hospital, he was fine. You could not sleep that night, nor many nights after. You kept seeing blood.

III. SKYWORLD

Last week, I played it again on your machine, my inheritance. It is impossibly hard. I keep falling. The reaper looks smug in his purple vestments. I whine whenever I'm injured. The creatures I slaughter leave behind blood-red hearts.

I cheated to get to the final battle: with a shield of mirrors, I keep firing beams of light into Medusa's eye. She does not particularly seem to care.

IV. THE PALACE IN THE SKY

I have two lasting visions of you. The first is a photograph of you and my brother. He is eight and has caught his first muskie. You are holding it for him: 43½ inches long. It is May, and not muskie season. He has to let it go.

The second is you standing in your living room, the shag carpet rusting beneath you. You have just said "Icky Kid!" then laugh a great Polish laugh.

V. UNDERWORLD

I do not sleep well at night. I have learned. What am I faking with these hands?

Grace. Whatever might approach artistry. Blood.

SUITE FOR TI-99/4A

HUNT THE WUMPUS

I wanted to be a cryptozoologist before I knew the word. The library had a whole shelf of books on mysterious creatures, their photographs grainy as twilight. I studied Loch Ness so that, upon reaching a lake, I could instantly discern a fish from a flipper, a mouth from a distant moor. In the woods behind our house, the trails seemed winding enough—thin strands of dirt that eventually knotted together. I had a crude snare of rope and a bag of meat as bait. But nothing caught, nothing ate. The bat in our bathroom was spooky enough until my father zipped it out of the air with a towel. He said some ducks were called helldivers, but my mother could prove the muddy prints in the back hall were mine.

MUNCH MAN

I wanted to be a chef, but I wouldn't eat potatoes. I wouldn't eat liver or beans. I wouldn't eat cheesecake. Broccoli. Lamb. Sloppy joes. Oranges. Peas. Bread with nuts in it. Polish, Italian, or breakfast sausages. Tomatoes. Plums. I wouldn't eat pumpkin pie. Who knows how I would have survived if my mother hadn't made the same lunch for me every school day, from first through twelfth grades: chicken nuggets in a pouch of tinfoil, an apple, pretzel rods snapped like pencils, maybe some chocolate or a cookie. Sometimes a note, like the one I remember: *M is for mother, I guess, not for maître d'.*

ALPINER

I wanted to be a mountaineer, stand someplace where the wind kept punching my face but everyone below was so small and far away. Instead, one June, I leapt off the deck with an umbrella, fracturing both it and my elbow. She drove me to the hospital while my eyes were awash in pain. She didn't say much as they wound my arm in a bandage until it became a sweaty worm, or at dinner as I learned to spear Salisbury steak with my other hand. That night, she tucked me in, kissed my head like a whisper, turned out the light. Closing the door, she said, "Sweetheart, try not to fall so fast."

MEGA MAN

The claptrap Washington County Fair: rabbits with lazy eyes, chickens stuck on cluck, ribbons tacked above cattle stalls offering their silken wind. My friend and I were talking the future. "All robots eventually go haywire," he said to me as we walked by the Scorpion, sparks shooting from one of its arms. A man stood by it, wielding his welding torch like a blue knife, his mask a mirror of stars.

But I didn't care about that. There was Rebecca, dark hair and cottony eyes, who went to another school, who called me Buster and meant it. The evening was cool, so I offered her the sweatshirt from my Mexican vacation and my arms thick as viola strings. We rode the Tilt-a-Whirl. The bumper cars. The Gravitron to see if centrifugal force could make our heads stop spinning.

It was like sleeping on a platform suspended by nothing.

Of course there was the Ferris wheel, operated by a carny with Ice Man tattooed on his bicep like a cattle brand. "Let's see if you have the guts," he said as his cigarette winked, so I kissed her at the top the way I threw a ping-pong ball to win her a goldfish—lots of ricocheting followed by a soft splash.

Her mother drove up and she slid into the car, the sweatshirt saying something about fun. My friend wanted to throw darts at balloons. I wanted to ask the fortune-telling machine, the gypsy mannequin staring into her dim bowling ball. But her hands were locked mid-omen, a seamstress whose scissors were exhausted from snipping up strips of people's wishes. A man twirled the cord like a cane while waiting for someone to cart it away. He could tell my hands were on fire. "Here, kid," he said, and handed me the card I tacked above my bed for what I swore would be forever:

Being an electrician is different than being a doctor of light.

GAUNTLET

In high school, how useful was it for me to be a wizard in calculus, or a thief who could only steal glances? As useful as a sharp wit in an axe fight. As useful as a tuning fork in a locker room. Back then, I was elfish as a miniature Elvis. Yet somehow I still dated a valkyrie, her breasts protected by steel plates and her mother's proclivity for being home at all the right times.

"Someone shot the food," I'd joke in the lunch line, then we'd take our seats in the cafeteria like two ghosts in a dungeon of ghouls. She had a key to her silver locket; I had a key to a car that would run only if the heat blew full force. Especially in summer.

Junior year I picked up some Latin as easily as a paper clip, but started swinging it around like a sword. *Carpe diem. Memento mori.* "This warrior is about to die," I'd say to her sixth period after braving the corridors all crammed with cliques. I said it regularly as a prayer.

One night, she answered: "I hear potions can kill death." Sixteen years later, I suppose she's still right. I can still smell the bargain-bin massage oil—jasmine and sandalwood floating atop a sweaty man smoking a cigar. Still feel the gray blanket with holes big as exit signs. Taste the rum dribbling down her neck to become a spray of gasoline pooling in her thighs.

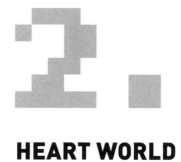

HEART WORLD

DONKEY KONG

Your boyfriend, m'lady, is drunk, hurling barrels down the hall of the barroom, offering many botched attempts at lighting your cigarettes. Your purse, your hat, your pink-and-white parasol could be anywhere. What is he yammering about with his chest-thumping? And you're calling too, from the rafters. When your boyfriend thinks the floor is falling beneath him and he drops, I check on you as I should. But it is love, love for me, I can tell by your Easter-pink heart.

A week later, m'lady, I stop at the bar after work. Your boyfriend seems even angrier now, spinning barrels down the baffled beams. As before, you look exquisite, but: your cries are off-key, and have the faint echo of shouting into an oil drum or walking a wheelbarrow through building after unfinished building.

MS. AND SUPER PAC-MAN

They met at Overeaters Anonymous. She liked his muscular mouth; he loved the sweet-sexy bow in her hair. They chased each other around a playground like school kids—her knees on a swing; his dizziness from the merry-go-round, staring at stars. She would make him fruit salad—bananas, strawberries the color of lipstick, apples, the soft flesh of a pear. He gave her the key to his neon apartment. They talked about having a child: a lemon growing from the size of a dot in her womb. Everything was comfortable as a good shoe.

Slowly, she wondered about being with someone who knew how to cut corners. He relapsed, guzzling donuts while she was at work. She once said, "No heart should be knotted like a pretzel"; he longed to lift the hem of another's orange dress.

—You surprised me when you said you wanted to try new things: amaretto sours, maybe ecstasy, flirting with the waiter who brought us our bottle of wine. You began with cigarettes, a cloud of coughs ghosting through the room. I would stand outside, contemplating the maze of sidewalks, wearing my coat like a cape in the rain.

ASTEROIDS

That August we watched the Perseids on the lake. I tried to impress you with the constellations I knew: a teapot, a bumblebee, Zeus with a lightning bolt, a jug of wine.

I was making them up.

*

You oohed when one whooshed large and low. I knew they were all space junk, God jizz, whore iron, star snot. I knew how much burning hurt.

Now you tell me a story. Tell me again how much you love me.

DOUBLE DRAGON

Our love was no dojo, I suppose: no moth on a bell in a temple, no statue with brass knuckles. You quickly learned my many buttons: leave this one locked in a shirt cuff; press this one for snarl, this one for laugh. You played them easily as a scale on your middle school flute.

Maybe it was the city: we tried to live as billboards for something better. But the walls were cracked and the cobblestone was creepy. There were shirtless men with muscles like mountains and women who wore spandex in nice places. Towards the end, maybe we should have tried whipped cream, barrels of booze, dynamite. But a conveyor can only carry so much.

It was New Year's Day. I had hung a photo of you with brown string, and I cut it down. I kicked a can until it was crushed and caroming off curbs, like my brother and I used to do. That night, in the blankness of my bunk bed, it hit me: the only person left to fight was myself.

ALTERED BEAST

Your ruthlessness made me grateful we prize rage: it was so easy. I became a werewolf snarling the traffic, a bear with claws like an egg slicer, a vodka-breathing dragon sizzling with electricity. You left me in Rockford when I got a flat tire. I kissed you on 27th Street but wanted to crush your cigarette on the back of your knee.

I did not need to die to claim I was undead. You did not need to coo "Two of Us" and say you were maligned as a dove. Evil will do what it will. The final photograph I burned was us in a group, heroes and villains all, holding our pints aloft in conviviality, frothy things.

I want to press a button clearly labeled HOIST A BEER. Let's sit down. Let's talk about this.

THE LEGEND OF ZELDA

It is human to expect narrative, to thread meaning. Your knees twinge in bed, your bruxism is tearing your teeth to powder, you swear you hear a train whistle and awake from stony sleep. Those seem connected enough. But: your cat had to be put to sleep, the tanning place charges $45 per month, the Pope died, your brother is driving inscrutably West, capital W.

Quick! Cut a roll of butcher paper to eleven inches wide, feed the scroll to your typewriter, hop yourself up on mescaline, tap it all down. Surely this is worth retelling. Here is the church; here is the steeple. Here is a scarlet tanager that flew into the stained glass windows.

I had the right things for you, and you didn't want them. A candle, a bracelet, a book. My spine ached. My clothes were so hip.

You said it in spite as you were leaving, and I didn't believe you until now: We become the stories we tell ourselves.

RAMPAGE

Alright, Peoria, I'm tired of this three-building town. The people shrieking like teakettles. The apothecary that glows in the dark. The riflemen shooting as if they were frosting a cake—nothing but petaled sugar.

In school, we've all seen movies about lizards, the way they sit still except for the rotating turrets of their eyes, until they unroll their tongue like a party favor at the funeral of some poor ant. We learn scientists pour questions into capsules, label them Eat Me, then tell us to report should we experience any answers. We know toasters and cigarettes both smoke.

O Peoria, don't you love St. Louis anymore? And what about that lovely little Davenport? The way its lock could talk for hours with your dam.

It's getting late, helicopters dragging dark netting behind them. Will I play in Peoria? Am I ready to rock? Because I only break two things on purpose:

My ex-lovers' windows. My future lovers' hearts.

MAP WORLD

THE OREGON TRAIL

We knew we'd have to buy provisions, so I tallied them on the back of a map: two columns of numbers like wagon ruts, us driving down a narrow road of coins. Who knows what we were hunting with our squirrelly eyes. You saw me take a marker and draw a buffalo-skull tattoo over my heart. We saw a herd of goats pontificating down a mountain like a derailed train. A bear's paw print the size of a steering wheel. The wind churning water to foam. You saw me wander down to Crazy Woman Creek and cry like dysentery until the world blurred blue.

Whatever we had, we mended. Or else we threw it away: the green camp stove that would take no more gas, careening like a shot parrot down a cliff.

A year later, you said you were moving to Portland. Said you were in love with Mt. Hood, the way its snowcap made it look like the ultimate covered wagon, a rugged place you might call home. By then, I had found someone willing to swim my tricky rivers. The ink on my chest evaporated, and now only you or I could ever trace the map of its scar.

POLE POSITION

Montana had no speed limit, but that didn't mean we believed the tobacco billboards. One read STEP RIGHT UP with a carnival flourish, a man swinging a cigarette like a sledgehammer, ringing a bell of smoke. YOU NEVER KNOW UNTIL YOU TRY said a woman in dark lingerie, extending the pack toward you until it looked like it might land in your lap. A third had the Savior, wire octagonal dipper, neon eggs, cups frothed with vinegar: JESUS DYED FOR YOUR SINS. The cigarette stuck in his mouth like a commandment.

"It began when she dyed her hair black," you said. "It began when I mistook her angles for curves," I said. Then we didn't say anything for a while. The clouds like a cough. The mountains jagged as a heartbeat. We blurred past cars that all looked the same.

I had a three-ring binder that caught paper like a Venus Flytrap, but I couldn't drive stick. I had a pen and a lighter to burn. I drew in a breath sharp as a stop sign then said a prayer of forgiveness. You were prepared for a long night of driving; I was prepared to qualify the truth.

JOURNEY

And so your battered scarab ferried us to a land of unearthly geologies. Love, we learned there, was whatever we found on the ground: broken shale atop a knife ridge, the glowing blue lozenge of the Saskatchewan Glacier, thrashing sounds from Sunwapta Falls. We were exuberant, flying mainly on instruments; our faces were invincible as album covers.

But: You got a speeding ticket in Manitoba. I fell asleep in Montana holding the map, causing you to take the wrong road. We blew a tire in Rapid City.

The land soon rolled, more familiar. The road slid over the river at La Crosse, then down. Love was whatever was on the radio—Beatles, Stones. So we sang along: something about *young,* something about *fly away.*

SINISTAR

By spring, I was sort-of reassembled. Through my broken jaw, all I could say was, "I hunger." It felt right, mistaking simplicity for depth. "I hunger," I told my friends, and they sent me to the Chat Noir for coffee and dessert crepes. "I hunger," I proclaimed from the top of Saylorville Dam, and the pelicans in the reservoir—pelicans in Iowa in April, how odd—guffawed with their full pouches. I ate the wind in South Dakota and it was dusty, all aces and eights. I said the hills at Buffalo Pound Provincial Park looked like buttered rolls. I was moving illogically quickly.

In August, I spat in Lake Winnebago. "Beware, I live," I sneered at the moorings. "Beware. I live," I called to the gulls. That was my real motto. I wanted to bleed it onto love letters, stitch it onto pillows, etch it into paperweights that would sit pointlessly on my papers, scrimshaw it onto her bones. "Beware, I live," I told you, as if it was the first half of an insidious palindrome: *Beware, I live; evil I, era web.*

ASTROSMASH

The second time I got drunk was during a certain uneven summer. My best friend was dating my childhood best friend. My girlfriend stayed in Des Moines, alternating bikinis and floods. I kept dreaming about Montana until it felt like glaciers gouged my eyes. There was a road called Going-to-the-Sun, so we went to town for some pizza.

I didn't know what good beer was then, but I was certain I'd never drink something called a Snake Bite. The second friend held my hand, holy, told me she was happy, said she'd like to get some coffee tomorrow morning. The first held a philosophy titled Thrust. The urinals seemed to vibrate. Entire horizons listed to port.

We went outside: gravel Wisconsin. "Look. The stars. Are changing colors," I said to them, then slumped in the back seat like a bag of bullets. The cornfields green as Venus. The billboards lonely as omens. And me with my fingers for pistols, shooting the moon.

FROGGER

Sometimes, in the closet of 3 a.m., I imagine the journey we didn't take. The go-kart track in Fargo where we slammed around corners as easily as swinging a stopwatch on its lanyard. The clouds slinking like submarines through the ocean of an Oklahoma sky. Otters in the Snake River. The girl in the sporting goods store in Cranbrook, British Columbia—purple dress, pink hair, a skull-and-crossbones tattoo on her ankle—standing between us and the fishing poles, saying, "It's all in the wrist, boys, it's all in the wrist."

Then I get out of bed, stand on the deck, look at the stars. The bullfrogs glunk their love songs to the moon. The grass blades gather beads for their morning tiaras of dew. Even the highway is done with driving for now.

I go back to bed, try dipping my toes in the river of sleep. I can almost picture the sunset over the Platte River we didn't see, ripe as a nectarine, or hear water churning like an engine in a ravine below while I straddle a fallen log.

Some things are too dangerous to cross.

HEART WORLD

QIX

This was in the town of rectangles.

I was a fuse, mistaking my hissing for whispers. You were a silver sphere, rolling long and low.

It was as if your calculus could complete us.

And so we went to the Italian restaurant, ate focaccia and wood-oven pizza. And so your bra was like your highlighter: hot and pink. And so my grandfather died three days before Easter.

At the funeral, the priest left out the part about resurrection. He didn't say cemetery plots are laid out like actuarial tables.

Yet when we laid in bed, straight and still as the symbol for parallel lines, the moonlight did what it could to fill in the gaps: our fenced pastures glowing electric blue.

DON'T GO ALONE

Chemistry is for people who hate table salt, you first told me, and I had to agree, since all I remembered from that corrosive subject was how much I loved its sounds: *molybdenum, ytterbium, Avogadro, Le Châtelier.* But what lead has to do with plumbing or radiation with sleight of hand is anybody's guess.

Those early years, our exotic new songs: *saguaro, saltimbocca, Okoboji, pizzadilla.* The scientists among us were astounded, calculators flummoxed with steam.

Then for a while I was crazy with fear. In my first house, the bedroom's hardwood floors were gap-toothed as gravel. Weekday midnights we'd creak the bed around like a gasping four-wheeled ghost ship.

But too often I laid there for days and could not get out. I could not get out. I was trying to write the right lonely sound, but mostly it was trucks jostling down West Avenue and a radio I imagined just out of earshot. The long and something road.

Our home has grown deeper. Our language is beautiful: *cat, garden, milk, table, school.* I come home at two in the morning smelling like smoke and I say *bar* and you say *sleep* and it is good.

Good luck, were your father's words, smiling, shaking my hand.

RIVER RAID

I never wanted to be a fighter pilot, although the explosions seemed fancy enough: pixellated shrapnel scattered like metal seeds. I never wanted to be a cruise ship captain, hobnobbing on the lido deck, knowing the terror of propellers as they gargled through the Caribbean at three in the morning.

Just because they called it the Skunk River doesn't mean we didn't fall in love in Iowa. Your eyes gray as Tuesday. My hands fluttering like rain while I slept. The words that ran through our lips, smooth and curled as oxbow lakes.

It's easy to say this now, lazing in northern Wisconsin. I have come in a canoe comfortable as a clamshell, yellow as a marsh marigold. The camp chair is settled in shale and iron-tinged water as I wave my pen like a baton, conducting this symphony of letters. Horseflies and damselflies. Minnows and crayfish. The grasses on the banks whisper of a distant storm while the cumuli build up like cauliflower.

Maybe I'd like to demolish the Bachelor's Avenue bridge so I could live here as the trees do: forever. Maybe I'd like to be a helicopter, hovering forever over the river of the body of you.

OUR YEAR IN ATARI

MEGAMANIA

"You have too many books," you said.
"I also have too many teeth," I said.

COMBAT

"Will you get me a glass of water?" you said.
"No," I said.

BOWLING

"You have a cute ass," I said.
"Thank you," you said.

BURGERTIME

"We don't need to eat at McDonald's. You're getting fat."
I did not respond.

PONG

"I love you."
"I love you, too."

FROGGER

"Perhaps we should try it like this," I said.
"Okay," you said.

ASTEROIDS

"The sky is falling," I said.
"It's just hail," you said.

CARNIVAL

"I still can't shoot out the red star," I said.
"No, you can't," you said.

RIDDLE OF THE SPHINX

"Do you know what I'd like?" you said.
"Does it start with an *m* and end in an *argarita*?" I said.

KABOOM!

"You never care about how *I* feel," you said.
"Fuck off," I said.

BURGERTIME

"What do you want me to make for dinner?"
You did not respond.

PONG

"I love you."
"I love you, too."

FREEWAY

"Wonder what happened," I said.
"I'll look; you just drive."

BUBBLE BOBBLE

The world was bright as candy.

I don't mean some halcyon youth. Rather the October when we were walking on the Ice Age Trail, the trees shooting off their fireworks of leaves, our son curled in your belly. I was saying something about how love is no amulet, a kiss is no magic, when I scuffed over a dinosaur bone, smooth and white as a dinner plate.

Brontosaurs trampling Wisconsin! Pangaea unzipping away! And now a whole skeleton beneath me, locked in a crypt of glacial loam!

It wasn't a dinosaur bone.

By then, it was now. Our living room an archaeology of toys. The plastic keys. The musical cube. A cell phone with four buttons that calls twinkling little stars. And he's learning a new trick with his saliva: bubbles on his lips like the domes in some strange spit city.

I met a stegosaur at the drugstore today. I wanted to ask her about her plates, about thermal regulation, about keeping the broth of her blood neither a ball nor a boil. About how you could love yourself, your mate, your child when you know you all came from eggs. But she didn't want to talk about any of that. Atop her head rode a seventy-nine-cent pink plastic bottle filled with soap water and the ridiculous ridged wand.

"Bubbles," she said. "I'm one hundred and forty-three million years old, and I still love blowing bubbles."

MANIAC MANSION

"This water is radioactive," you said to me when we first bought our house. "It tastes like Marie Curie's sweat." I tried to say no, tried to explain the iron in the well as railroad spikes left after the locomotive of a glacier, but by then some windows were cracked because I sing like an alien mating call.

We'd call it a money pit if we had any. Yet somehow, we've scraped toward respectability: the carpets can be cleaned because I can move furniture. The wallpaper in the back hall was molting until we scored it off, to be replaced by a paint named Gypsy Red. It looked like a bucket of blood.

And now our son is sleeping in the next room. So far, he only laughs in his sleep—a splash of staccato tweets—because if the dark isn't funny, nothing is. At 3 a.m., I wander the house, singing lullabies that all seem to have the word *drunk*, although only Pepsi populates the fridge.

And now he's rustling like a calendar in a breeze. We haven't begun discussing what we should teach him. Maybe: a termite is a slave to its wood. Maybe: *Inns are not residences*. Maybe: don't pull the cat; don't put the hamster in the microwave. Things like that.

It is good to be known by the metropolis of dandelions in the yard. It is good to drink luminescence until your smile glows in the dark.

EXCITEBIKE

Mothers love helmets; fathers love bruises is an aphorism no one's invented. My brother calls from heliboarding in Alaska, where he was clocked at 78 mph. He says speed is the color blue but tastes like iron. My father, recovering from cancer, jumps off a cliff into the Sturgeon River, and even the beer-drinking teens are amazed.

Sure, you've heard this story: my grandfather bought me my first bike for Christmas. And there I was: wobbling the training wheels in serpentine tracks, capsizing in the slush of 115th Street. Then my friends and I built dirt ramps in the woods and they're still there, eroding like sad effigies of age ten.

My mother often said, "Eat every carrot and pea on your plate," and soon enough my wife is teaching our son how to shake his rattle, and he's so excited his arms flail in spastic semaphore. He will want a dirt bike and some mud through which to ride it. He will want a camera crew. And I will sit in the stands clutching my bubble wrap, worrying it in my fingers like rosary beads, popping a cell for each lap he makes.

DO WORLD

THE INCREDIBLE MACHINE

These cat-and-mouse days, it's all about equilibrium and physics. For every action, there's someone who'll complain about it. It's not the heat, it's the humidity; it's not the humidity, it's the parchment nest of wasps breathing under the eaves of your house, some hexagonal math problem gone screwy.

Sure, you could take drugs. The elderly do it all the time, and look how happy they are: bowling-ball eyes and hands like dead fish. Or you could dissect a stick of dynamite to find out how much is trinitrotoluene and how much is God. None of this will cure your alarm clock. Better to root for the tailor with his shears, entering a room of balloons tied to the triggers of guns.

MR. DO!

I dated a gypsy fruit picker for a while. Her palms creased with dirt. An accidental flower in her hair. Her scarves scented strawberry.

She taught me how to juggle with apples. My first dozen became bruised as the steamer trunk she dragged around with her like a dead albatross. But I got better. She taught me the trick where you toss one over your shoulder. The one where you take a bite mid-air. The one where you finish by catching one on the back of your neck. Soon, I graduated to crystal balls. All those futures flying from my hands.

"To be is to do," she said each morning as she sighed out of bed. To her, the orchards were like a tarot deck whose only suit was swords. "No breathing is easy," I would say, still lying down, stretching out, watching the harlequin morning. The sun a red clown nose, the dinosaurs still sleeping beneath shale, the freeway juggling thousands of cars.

ELEVATOR ACTION

In the interview room are many men in black suits, black fedoras. They are seated at boardroom tables, faces lit with mahogany gleam. You are called to the front, beneath a stark light. You are asked to state your business, release your files, completely fill in each circle, recite a poem you learned as a child.

I've had jobs where I could have ridden the elevators all day if I wanted to: harmonizing their hum, figuring their numbers. Thirteen times thirteen times thirteen and I'd have a cube of unluckiness, another gewgaw to display on my desk.

You'd like to feel sorry as you pick them off one by one, but their eyes are dead squares and their mouths so worn out they've gone missing. The lights fluoresce and flicker. The Pacific Ocean sighs and heaves. As their lives become thinner than asterisks, you imagine they have the same final thought: *Who'll make sure the elevators run?*

SPACE INVADERS

They are coming in very well-organized rows. They bring knowledge of socialism, red airships, rock and roll, and the squiggle.

Children, quick! Only you can save suburbia! We will give you science classes, automobiles with ridiculous appendages, and countries in southeastern Asia.

Today the rain sifted through the lilacs. The sky was gray and fine as a dying man's hair. The wind told quiet stories.

We will give you an insurance middle-management position. We are helping people. We only take a little for ourselves. We will give you a pair of cardboard glasses with cellophane lenses, one red and one blue, so things appear to be in three dimensions.

DIG DUG

The exterminators wouldn't give me the job. The man explained it to me in his dingy office, a model of a termite colony on his desk, a poster of an ant with scythe-like fangs. "The only thing you've killed is houseflies," he said. "Anyone can do that," and he did, yanking one out of the air and mashing it between his fingers and palm. They wanted someone who knew how to make gas clouds swirl, how to draw a halo of chemicals around a house with a hose, how to incinerate wings. The man folded a page of the want ads into a paper airplane, sailed it, then exploded it with a small torch. "See?" he said.

Now the air is a thick soup of mosquitoes. I cook brats on the grill; I'm good at inflating balloons for parties. The way they jewel a ceiling like larvae. My wife leaves the spiders to their corners and won't touch the millipedes the cats torment.

I would just as soon we let the living go on living. An old poet whom we believe in said the same thing, said an old poet whom we'd like to believe in. A good job is hard to man. Maybe one day my shovel will hit something other than stone. Maybe soon the wasps whose nests are ballooning beneath the siding will pick up our house, sail it to the sky, their wings diaphanous as dragon scales. The clouds cooking something up.

Instead, I'll wake tomorrow, maybe make a little coffee. Then begin the work of sweeping away the mayflies that have fallen like dead angels all around our front door.

WHERE IN THE RETIREMENT HOME IS CARMEN SANDIEGO?

Thorp, Wisconsin: a few streets scratched within fields quilted by cows. At first, she wanted an apartment long and tall to keep her mementoes. The Statue of Liberty. The Strait of Magellan. Half of the fish from Lake Titicaca in their ridiculous bowl; the salt from the Dead Sea in its shaker.

But the manager didn't have anything like that. Instead, she moved into a unit like all the rest: a comfortable one-bedroom, beige carpet and beige walls. At the town rummage sale she sold the St. Louis Arch to a car dealer. Said he was going to spray-paint it blue, maybe tie on some balloons. Jazz it up. She's kept one lesser-known Rembrandt behind a cheap portrait of deer in a field. At night, she unscrews the frame, removes the top print, looks at the painting, then sighs.

Of course she lives under an alias, a normal one, not like all her accomplices. Polly Esther Fabrique. Mel Ancholy. Heidi Gosikh. Cal Q. Leytor. And the lovely Sarah Nade, piano teacher/punk rocker, a scar on her ear the shape of New Jersey. All either in prison or executed in a desert. She reads magazines, plays bridge. Lunches with her sewing circle at the Thorpedo. But she still wears sunglasses—after living in 256 colors for so long, she has to acclimate to all the world's nuance.

Lately, the police have grown suspicious. A fedora flew from a garbage can like an old owl. Calvin Coolidge's baby shoes appeared in the window of a thrift store, silent as ever. A velvet glove stopped up a storm drain on Main Street. And those high-heeled footprints in the first snow...

They are coming. They are coming and raiding the building. Flashlights and walkie-talkies. Barking dogs. The world is holding its breath. It wants the pieces of itself back. They are clomping down the stairs, down a hallway. They are throwing open the back door, rounding a corner...

A woman in an orange dress planting tulip bulbs in the frost.

6.

MIND WORLD

LOOM

The 1983 Halloween, I was the red Pac-Man ghost. My mom made the costume, dyed it a color named Wine and stitched the squiggles of its agitated face all akimbo.

In 1986, she stood ironing in our brown living room. The TV was on. The *Challenger* had exploded. They kept showing it again and again, a perennial flowering of fire.

I took pictures of swans with her camera during the spring of 1992. It was as if they had risen from ice, bobbed for a while, then flew away.

In 1972, she and my dad smoked dope they called Wauwatosa Wacko.

Tonight, she invited Erin and me to dinner. Erin was going to aerobics. I was going to drink and write with my friends. We had already eaten dinner. Erin is at aerobics. I am writing and drinking with my friends.

In 1997, I told her the quarter-moon cut me like a scythe. It was the one thing she wished she had told me sooner.

PERFECT DARK

We love our crooked minds, but find them unmappable, *terra incognita*. The rain is eating away the stone. Our clothes do not match our bodies.

We rummage for any apt metaphor. Perhaps it is seeing through many walls, in heat vision, the others running down angular hallways. Perhaps it is setting up a thought that will obliterate all thoughts that come thereafter. Perhaps it is crisp electricity in your hand, ten poison-tipped knives, the recoil of a silver revolver.

It is none of these things.

We do, however, know how to kill people, and lustily so: their flesh is fodder for our love. We are mercilessly efficient—no remorse for those hapless cartographers.

You find a crate of neutron bombs and lob one into a small room. It is perfect. There is a flash and an ineffable sound: it sucks every energy inward, amorphous and black. The others stumble, are dizzy and blurred, gasp and fall to the ground. You throw another and the nebula grows. You cackle, pitching another and another, and then: an artful stroll amidst the buzzing darkness.

RAD RACER

You are driving west at manic speeds. To distill driving to the purity of elements, you say: road, car, desert, sign, scrub. Distant San Francisco is neon phantasms, look how they float. At times, you close your eyes for lengthy stretches, the way a Zen archer shoots at night.

—What are you trying to do? *Nothing, man. Just driving.*

MARBLE MADNESS

The patient does not understand the diagnosis, so the doctor tries again: "Imagine you are a blue marble seeking a taste of tableau" (he levels the air with a flat sweeping palm), "but all you see are ramps and hillocks, impossible canyons and fescue-strewn ravines. Also, there is a black marble always orbiting, which snarls and gnashes whenever it swings near. But" (and here he hooks his thumbs together and makes a flitting gesture), "the black marble *isn't really there.*" Satisfied, the doctor sits back, then reaches behind the patient to produce a glass of water that morphs through colors. He drinks it in a slug, and sets the glass on the edge of his desk, glistening. The patient hears an occasional ting of a bell, but looks at the glass again and finds it is slowly shattering, each shard dropping like a diseased petal.

ICE CLIMBER

Say the mind is a mountain.

That's easy enough: worn trails of habits, purple vultures that sail, cliffs where questions hang like icicles. The wind really slapping the clouds of thought around.

O despair! O brokenheart! O death!

Say there is someone ascending that mountain, blue parka and titanium ice axe, chipping out chunks of brain, level by level. Crampons. Pitons. Carabiners. A Peruvian hat with balls dangling from either side.

Now we're getting somewhere.

Say as a child you never ate your vegetables, eggplants and carrots staring right at you. So now you take vitamins, a whole alphabet crammed into the word of a capsule. *A* for your eyes. *D* for your skin. Iron to rust your sweat. Neon to appear bright. Each pill is a communion and a penance.

And now the climber is approaching the summit. He's eating a protein-based goo. He's drunk on the oxygen he's been lugging around in tanks like torpedoes. He's made of proprietary hydrochlorides. He's sculpting then sleeping in a quinzhee.

And he's hammering the hell out of the gray, spongy snow, trying, desperately trying, to make you happy.

DOOM

Luck favors the prepared: yet another reason why I'm an atheist. Sometimes in a conversation, someone needs to know the date Lincoln was assassinated. The chemical components of methane. The difference between a diatonic and pentatonic scale. I smile and just stand there, blank as a summer blackboard.

Because when I sleep, my brain is hellbent on clearing out clutter, killing useless facts as if they were mutants. Goodbye, Prometheus stole fire from Mt. Olympus. Farewell, the capital of Portugal is Lisbon. Differential equations, I hardly knew ye.

If it gets hold of a rocket launcher or chain gun, my brain can mow down whole columns of data: the rulers of Britain or Saturn's moons. All that's left is pixellated blood where the neurons were, dendrites spitting out sparks. My brain wants its caverns clean until only secrets like knickknacks line its shelves.

I wonder what God thinks of me, if He thinks of me at all.

THE SECRET OF MONKEY ISLAND

It's not faith. God is everywhere: in the jailer, voodoo charms, your hands. Ask the tongues of fire lapping up their logs. Ask the blind man, and he will smell it. Ask the deaf man, and he will sing you a psalm.

It's not music. You can beat on the table or yodel while swinging from a chandelier. Here's a note; here's a chord. Here's a staff for you to walk through the woods, the wind and you both whistling.

It's not money. Soon enough it all sinks in the sea. There are chests seized with salt, there are shovels and maps, and there are Xs on your grandmother's cross-stitching that hangs in your hallway. On the back, only her signature and a year once engraved on pennies and which you know little about.

It's not love, honey pumpkin. The pirates are wedded to their grog, the trees to their roots. Everyone knows that, sugar boots. Did your mother once buy you a pair of wax lips in the drugstore when you were five? Of course she did, fuzzy bunny.

It's not death. You can swing a sword in an arc and hold your breath underwater if you must. What are you going to do once interred, stare still and think *decompose*? It's coming as certain as a comet. Watch the sky.

It's not the moon, mooring in the wharf of your eyes.

Here's a secret: about the big things, most people are terrified most of the time. It brings us together, and that is good, little monkey-faced, sweet-muffin, jumping-bean babies of mine.

DARK WORLD

PAC-MAN

At five, I wanted to believe in ghosts.

A man who had lived in my room, my parents told me, was caught in a storm on the lake, hair now standing shocked for eternity. But Wisconsin summers when the thunder marched in, hushing the thrum of crickets, the lightning was ridiculous as a flashbulb, like the moon throwing a surprise party but too dumb to know when to stop yelling *Surprise*.

Then this game, ghosts adorable as orphans, raveling clothes and blue eyes lolling around their big heads. Stammering through blank alleys at night.

O Inky, Pinky, Blinky, and Clyde: Who is God? What is death? Where is Wisconsin? Are you my mother?

A farm was a mile away by bike, corn and cows. I wanted to keep touching that electric fence.

Q*BERT

Cartoon characters needn't fear ledges. It's beautiful here in the desert: mesas built up like pyramids, rattlesnakes coiled in cool, a pinyon jay cackling in the pines. All day, our hero has been chasing or chased, as the script requires, overshoots the lip of a cliff, and soon he is skittering on air. He floats long enough to hold up a sign with a funnypage swear—a riot of asterisks and exclamation points—and then comes the descending whistle, the splat. Below, he gets up and shakes the dust from his hair, but otherwise no claw, paw, or bone out of place.

Step right up, folks, into this carnival of life: a cacophony of colors, flashing lights, a juggler with a cascade of rubber balls, spinning things. Step right up to the edge, peer over, contemplate the vastness below and the silver ribbon of a river tied beneath it. Step right up, pay a quarter, win a prize. You sir, yes, you sir. Mister Muscles. You look like a man who could ring gravity's bell.

GRIM FANDANGO

I.

Not dumbfounding bliss, nor pointless and cruel, we learn death is creepily familiar: bureaucracy, small-scale flirting, yearning. Occasional cloisters of comrades, a gaudy festival, liquor with flecks of gold in the bottle. Memoranda, more yearning, and bones. But there, everything is more stylish, with muted colors in the patchwork windows, cigarette cases and holders, and the rounded architecture saying: *Above all, we need to be smooth.*

II.

We were the two people you knew who wouldn't mind being dead, you said, and yet: here we were. I laughed, then you laughed; we found it funny, and it *was* funny. Most things are funny when you wouldn't mind being dead.

III.

Nunca he pedido más que un pájaro hecho de huesos. Tienen la música más hermosa aquí. Cuando duermo, sueño que puedo tocar la nieve mientras cae en las flores, y cuando me despierto, todos los trenes se levantan para saludarme.

You said this to me in your sleep.

KING'S QUEST

The only good fairy tales are fatal: witches in cauldrons, a giant like some unholy hailstone, the wolf belching out a red bonnet. Forget the narcoleptic princess, the adjectival dwarves. Four-and-twenty blackbirds baked in a pie and you'll die eating crow.

Mirror, mirror, all you've told me this past week is the sixth gray hair. If I stuck a feather in my cap, what would you call it? —Denial.

Too often I hate the kingdom bequeathed to me, mountains murdered by glaciers. The barred owl behind Fox Hill asks, "Who cooks for you?" and I say, "Tonight I'm making Chicken Kiev for Erin." Off Cty Hwy NN, the rotting trees in the swamp freeze like astonished soldiers. Draco won't breathe unless I blow cigarette smoke to the sky. The sun blinks like popped bubble gum each evening and all I can think of is missing her even though she's in the next room.

My mother once gave me a sachet with a three-masted clipper printed on it, something to put in your sock drawer, that also said *I love you!* At baby showers, they melt candy bars into diapers. At funerals, everyone is so clean. So dearie, fetch me my dustpan. Someone needs to sweep up these breadcrumbs.

SMASH TV

It took me fifteen years to learn this: everyone on TV is duplicitous.

Game show hosts wear sport coats sewn of moonlight. Their blood bubbles neon. They have a lovely home version.

If *you take the good, you take the bad, you take them both: there you have* notes dumb as rabbits, their stems snared in traps. *Streaks on the china never mattered before. Who cares?*

It took me fifteen years to learn this: no one cares if you die.

High school teaches this, mostly: the isotopes of carbon with their long and mournful half-lives; the skull of a fetal pig snipped open like cardboard, revealing a brain, a labyrinth of questions.

But I was never one to look at the spaces between stars.

Sometimes, when I lay down at night, it feels like I'm on a boat, a sick rocking. Each night, my ears ring, which is not normal. Each night, my eyes see static in the dark like snow on a TV. Which is not normal. The afterimages are all pastel cool. In dreams, I play the home version of myself: grass, water, wife, friends.

It took me thirty years to learn this: the only thing you can't dream is sleep.

TEMPEST (BY WAY OF WORMS)

Everyone is suspicious of animals that live underground: gophers grinding up gardens, a snake coiled in its ball of dirt until spring. Catch a skunk in its burrow and it's like lightning stinking up the night.

Consider the worm: no hardhat for its head, the gizzard its lunchbox. After strong storms, they sulk on the sidewalks, helpless as noodles. They're soil churning through soil, a small slice of slime for the robins, an etymology lesson on *annular* they didn't ask for; yet they are pistons pumping an immense network of tubes, paid only by fallen leaves. They can't call in airstrikes or drive tanks. They don't ask for more than they were given.

Soon we will send a spaceship to Mars. There, the crew will be frightened of everything: the strange sky, the crooked canals, the spikes on their boots in the rusted soil and whatever might be beneath them. But most of all they will fear the compartment of animals they had to bring: worms for their red crops, and the cages of flies, rats, coyotes, and crows.

JOUST

At the ostrich farm, each is first given a clever name: Flyboy. Flapjack. Eggciting Eggbert. Ostrichlopithecus.

Then they are given a bridle, the nice kind. Leather, soft and chewy. Almost like licorice, really.

Then they are given knights and a battle. It is the highest ostrich honor to be martyred. But most wind up flocking to the coast to convalesce: tail feathers bruised as an oil slick; a broken claw hanging from a toe, bugling its song of pain.

Then they are given a god, which is actually a rubber pterodactyl—the kind you bought at a drugstore and flew around the living room when you were ten. But to them, it's an awesome, slavering thing: scales like bronze shields, and each of its screams is a lava commandment. It skims the air like an aria; it dresses in vestments of their fallen feathers.

Then they are given two prayers. The first is a long lamentation beseeching forgiveness. The second recants everything said in the first.

Years pass.

Then they are returned to the farmer, who wears overalls yellow as corn. He hasn't seen them in ages, and they've grown succulent with sin. Folks gotta eat.

—O Flyboy. My sweet Flapjack. Poor old Eggciting Eggbert. Make a single-file line, quickly now, children. It is time now, children. It is time.

LIGHT WORLD

TEENAGE MUTANT NINJA TURTLES

I.

It was, of course, a smash with adolescent boys: you are a teenager, you are a freak, you have superpowers. You love pizza. You must rescue a girl–a girl!–and she will be grateful and love you eternally. Her name is April–April the month of wetness, fertility, and blossom. Her hair is strawberry blonde and her clothes tulip-yellow.

II.

A turtle's belief system is complex and still largely unknown. They suck in the sun, of course, but bay at the moon. You have heard them. Bullfrogs are the mothers of rains. Their altars are outlandish things, dodecahedral domes of mud and trash underwater. Turtle nirvana is not what you would expect: a green universe, a green emptiness with infinitely falling turtles, each catching conversation with whoever glides by.

III.

We are here again, playing the same damn game. We have our girls. We are eating pizza. What has changed?

–God, as impossible as it seems.

GOD PLAYS TETRIS

His machine is immaculate: gold and titanium, diamond resistors, and a seraphic hum while running. But the program, invented by Alexey Pajitnov and ported to the arcade by Atari in 1988, is the same.

The first levels are mindless, and He drops through them with Zen. Then: disembodied blocks, but it's easy, building towers with a dark canyon on one side, occasionally eroding it with the one straight piece.

Soon the shapes drift from virga to flurries to snow. A mislaid piece and He can still recover, without grace. Then muttering: "I'll put this square here, thank you; No, I don't want another six of those orange S-shaped pieces; Dammit, I just need a straight one"—which either does or does not come: His omniscience is useless.

Towers become ugly jumbled mountains, hard and fast. He has made mountains before and He has made floods, but His past sins will not wash away. He is drowning in squares. This is what it must feel like.

He loses, beats the side of the machine with His palm, wonders why He gave them free will. Well, it's not just this, but a lot of things. Unhip. Weary.

Then He exhales a laugh with a thin smile: He had forsaken Russia many years ago, so lurid: those creepy nesting dolls, any czarocracy, vodka, that Siberian nothing, communism, unnecessary quantities of potatoes, backwards Rs, atheists, and garish spindled minarets no holy man would enter.

BREAKOUT

When you see your first rainbow, you can only think variations of *wow*. It is a harmony of light, an impossible flower of colors seeded by rain. Soon enough, the sun begins to chip away the clouds, and it is gone. Soon enough come the lies about leprechauns. Soon enough, you learn rainbows are everywhere, common as coins: locked in the spray of a hose, pooled in a puddle of spilled gasoline, a whole confetti of them thrown on a wall by a crystal hung in a window. Then some science teacher will come and dissect them unhappily as frogs.

Now when I see one, I don't think *Thank God that storm has passed*. Instead I look for other half-circles: the green parabola of the ball while I'm losing at tennis, or the rainbow of dirt under my fingernails after I've been weeding.

Poor Noah. The ship creaking, rank with animals and their excrement. The sheep always bleating at the wolves. The penguins sweating and camels freezing. The giraffes that had to thread their necks out portholes, sullenly sodden. And forty days of this. What did he think, when he saw that rainbow? That it was the mouth of God come to devour him, frowning at all his failures?

GRAND THEFT AUTO: VICE CITY

I am born into this fecund garden, everywhere with flowering pastels: a perpetual Easter. The culture here is quickly acquired: how cool the brass knuckles ring round my fingers; how cool the breeze from the helicopter traversing the aquamarine inlets; how cool to be cool on Christ. At my gesture, your head explodes and your neck erupts a fountain of blood. It's a miracle.

At 6:07 I stood on the beach and watched the sky twinge from incandescent yellow to carnation pink to a smooth teal. At 12:17 I picked up my profit from the strip club: thank you, seraphic dancers; thank you, panting gentlemen, you're saints. At 18:30, I offered lessons to the Cubans about devotionals, vespers, and jihad. At 23:33, I stood at the apex of the interisland bridge. Arms winged open, bullets from the SWAT helicopter burning through my palms: "I forgive you," I whispered, and fell forward, below.

The next morning, I wash up at the Ocean View Hospital. It is a bright cloudless morning, tourists and commuters, everywhere with flowering pastels.

PSALM: GOLDENEYE 007

In a vast field of white, You are the orange sky.

In a room of computers, You are a scientist with his silver flask of wine.

A knife in a sewer, the underground traffic of mice, the deteriorating orbit and yaw—

You have my dossier. I surrender my weapons—

I want Your laser to burn through my bones.

SHARK! SHARK!

To describe the soul, begin with an empty ocean, and you in the middle of it, small as a sunbeam. Soon enough, other things come along: fish, bubbles in their glittering columns, the sediment of the seabed with its long encyclopedia entry on erosion. But how to grow?

"It's a god-eat-god world," says the cynic. "Neither the swimmer nor the shark," says the sage. "The forecast for Hell is still hot," says the weatherman. "We only know how to roll," say the waves.

Seahorses curly as questions.

Ask any third grader: What lunch do fish bring to school? Peanut butter and jellyfish sandwiches. What do crabs use for money? Sand dollars. What fish do you most want to be when you grow up?

God help you if you never said Angel.

GAME OVER

CONGRATULATIONS, ENTER YOUR INITIALS

At last, you've done it. After years of errors, oodles of maneuvers. You've baffled the bullets. Crossed every chasm. Bludgeoned all the bumblers until you became beatified. Congratulations.

When you were born, your mother cast upon you three letters like runes. All along, you've scrutinized them like a scholar, wondering when they might start spelling something sensible. Something more than a sweatshirt, an old car that needs new brakes, frozen pizza. Maybe even jealous of those who have *Ignatius* or *Makepeace* or *Magdalena*.

Now think of all the luminaries likewise initialed! Actresses. Philosophers. Explorers. Kings and queens. And Jesus Holy Christ, who has been atop the leaderboard for centuries. Now you are among them, your initials glorious, forever electric in their pantheon.

GAMES REFERENCED

Many of these games were released for multiple platforms, at multiple times, on multiple continents, and sometimes by multiple publishers. The information below gives the copyright year and publisher for each game's initial wide-scale North American release when known. If that information is not available, the game's initial publisher and/or year are used. The location of the publisher's headquarters at the time of the release is given when known; otherwise, its most recent location is used.

Alpiner. Dallas: Texas Instruments, 1982.
Altered Beast. Tokyo: Sega, 1988.
Asteroids. Sunnyvale: Atari, Inc., 1979.
Astrosmash. El Segundo: Mattel, 1981.
Bowling. Sunnyvale: Atari, Inc., 1979.
Breakout. Sunnyvale: Atari, Inc., 1976.
Bubble Bobble. Tokyo: Taito, 1986.
BurgerTime. Tokyo: Data East, 1982.
Carnival. Tokyo: Sega, 1980.
Combat. Sunnyvale: Atari, Inc., 1977.
Commander Keen in "Invasion of the Vorticons." Garland: Apogee, 1990.
Dig Dug. Sunnyvale: Atari, Inc., 1982.
Donkey Kong. Kyoto: Nintendo, 1981.
Don't Go Alone. San Jose: Accolade, 1989.
Doom. Mesquite: id Software, 1993.
Double Dragon. Tokyo: Taito, 1987.
Duck Hunt. Kyoto: Nintendo, 1985.
Elevator Action. Tokyo: Taito, 1983.

Excitebike. Kyoto: Nintendo, 1985.

Freeway. Santa Monica: Activision, 1981.

Frogger. Tokyo: Sega, 1981.

Gauntlet. Milpitas: Atari Games, 1985.

Golden Axe. Tokyo: Sega, 1989.

GoldenEye 007. Twycross: Rare, 1997.

Grand Theft Auto: Vice City. New York: Rockstar Games, 2002.

Grim Fandango. San Francisco: LucasArts, 1998.

Hunt the Wumpus. Dallas: Texas Instruments, 1980.

Ice Climber. Kyoto: Nintendo, 1984.

The Incredible Machine. Fresno: Sierra On-Line, 1992.

Journey. Franklin Park: Bally Midway, 1983.

Joust. Waukegan: Williams, 1982.

Kaboom! Santa Monica: Activision, 1981.

Kid Icarus. Kyoto: Nintendo, 1986.

King's Quest. Armonk: IBM, 1983.

The Legend of Zelda. Kyoto: Nintendo, 1986.

Loom. San Francisco: LucasFilm Games, 1990.

Maniac Mansion. San Francisco: LucasFilm Games, 1987.

Marble Madness. Sunnyvale: Atari Games, 1984.

Mega Man. Osaka: Capcom, 1987.

Megamania. Santa Monica: Activision, 1982.

Mr. Do! Tokyo: Universal, 1982.

Ms. Pac-Man. Franklin Park: Midway, 1981.

Munch Man. Dallas: Texas Instruments, 1982.

The Oregon Trail. Brooklyn Center: MECC, 1985.

Pac-Man. Franklin Park: Midway, 1980.

Perfect Dark. Twycross: Rare, 2000.

Pole Position. Sunnyvale: Atari, Inc., 1982.

Pong. Sunnyvale: Atari, Inc., 1972.

Q*bert. Chicago: Gottlieb, 1982.

Qix. Tokyo: Taito, 1981.

Rad Racer. Tokyo: Square, 1987.

Rampage. Franklin Park: Bally Midway, 1986.

Riddle of the Sphinx. Los Gatos: Imagic, 1982.

River Raid. Santa Monica: Activision, 1982.

The Secret of Monkey Island. San Francisco: LucasArts, 1990.

Shark! Shark! El Segundo: Mattel, 1982.

SimCity. Emeryville: Maxis, 1989.

Sinistar. Waukegan: Williams, 1982.

Smash TV. Waukegan: Williams, 1990.

Space Invaders. Franklin Park: Midway, 1978.

Super Mario Bros. Kyoto: Nintendo, 1985.

Super Pac-Man. Franklin Park: Bally Midway, 1982.

Teenage Mutant Ninja Turtles. Buffalo Grove: Ultra Games, 1989.

Tempest. Sunnyvale: Atari, Inc., 1980.

Tetris. Moscow: Various publishers, 1984.

Where in the U.S.A. Is Carmen Sandiego? Novato: Brøderbund, 1985.

Where in the World Is Carmen Sandiego? Novato: Brøderbund, 1985.

Worms. Manchester: Ocean Software, 1995.

ABOUT THE AUTHOR

B.J. BEST is the author of two previous books of poetry: *Birds of Wisconsin* (New Rivers Press) and *State Sonnets* (sunnyoutside). He is also the author of three chapbooks from Centennial Press, most recently the prose poem collection *Drag: Twenty Short Poems about Smoking.* He teaches at Carroll University and lives in the Wisconsin countryside with one wife, one son, three cats, and nine video game systems. He asserts he is the only person in the history of the world to have beaten *Super Mario Bros.*—with an actual Nintendo and television—on a pontoon boat.

A NOTE ABOUT THE TYPE

The body text of *But Our Princess Is in Another Castle* is set in Rotis Serif. Part of the highly varied Rotis family, it was developed by German typographer Otl Aicher, who named it after the German town where he lived. It was released by Agfa foundry in 1988—incidentally, a few years after the game *Tetris* was created in Russia. In the following decade rights to Rotis were acquired by Monotype Imaging. Rotis Serif has thick, heavy serifs, and there's a strong contrast between its thick and thin strokes. It's easy to read at small sizes like a classic book face should be, but it has a fresh, updated feel that sets it apart.

The interior display text is set in FF DIN Pro, an incarnation of DIN 1451. DIN began as a set of hand-drawn Prussian railway lettering in 1905, which served as the inspiration for the D. Stempel AG foundry's 1923 version of DIN. Germany adopted the typeface in 1936 as a standard font for public markers such as traffic signs and house numbers, and named it DIN 1451. A clear, legible face with a modern feel, FF DIN was developed by Albert-Jan Pool in 1995 and is currently owned by the FontShop foundry.

The typefaces used on the cover are also Rotis Serif and FF DIN Pro.

—HEATHER BUTTERFIELD